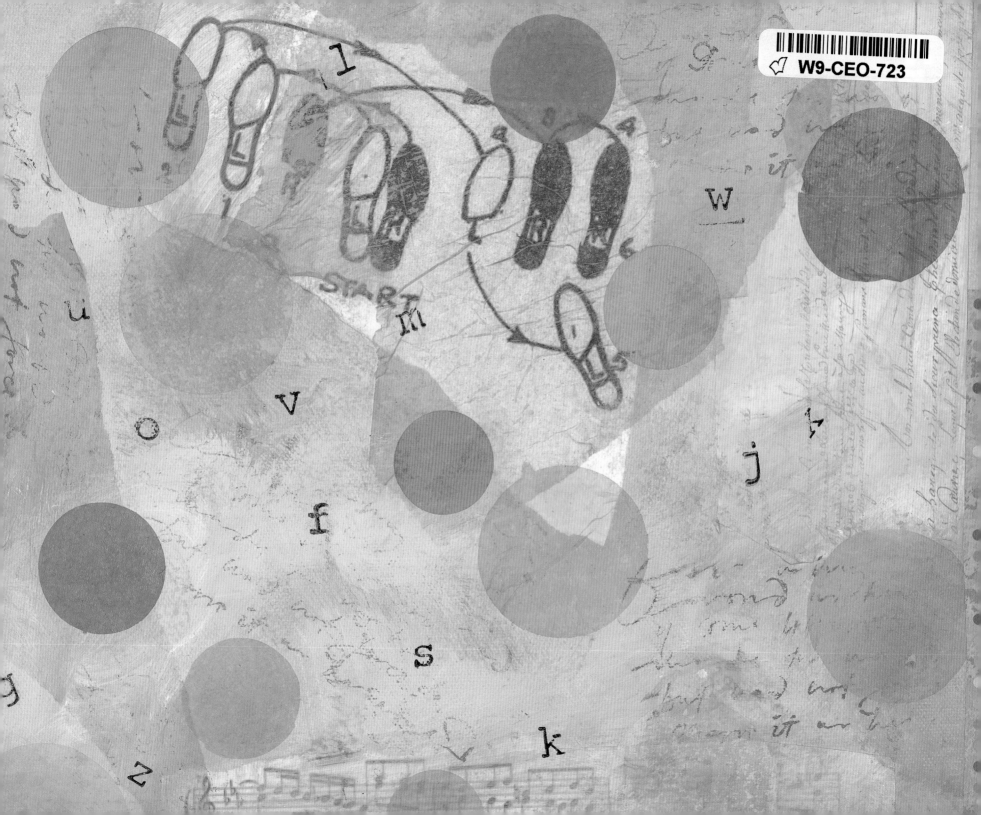

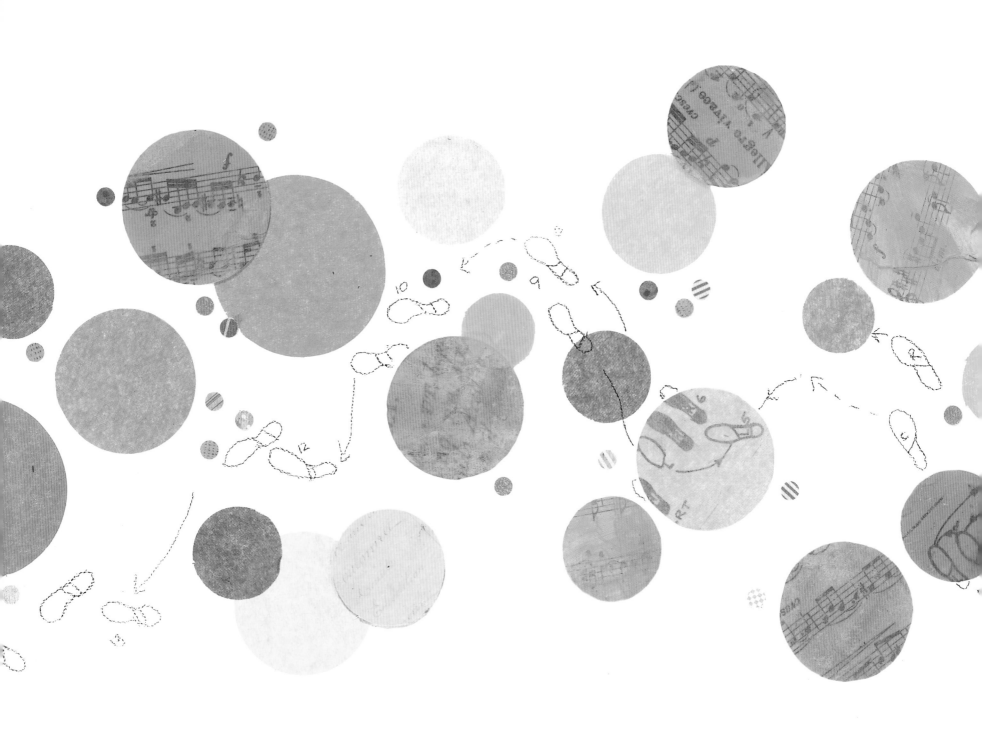

A Dictionary of DANCE

Liz Murphy

BLUE 🍎 APPLE

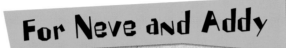

For Neve and Addy

Published in the United States 2012 by
Blue Apple Books
515 Valley Street, Maplewood, NJ 07040
www.blueapplebooks.com

Printed in China

ISBN: 978-160905-142-6

3 5 7 9 10 8 6 4 2

Arabesque

Arabesque (*a-ruh-BESK*)
a position in which the dancer stands on
one leg, straight or bent, with the other
leg extended backward

Break dancing (*brayk DANS-ing*)
fast dancing in which parts of the body
(arms, legs, stomach) touch the floor

Choreographer

Choreographer
(*kor-ee-AH-gruh-fur*)
person who creates the steps
to be used in a dance

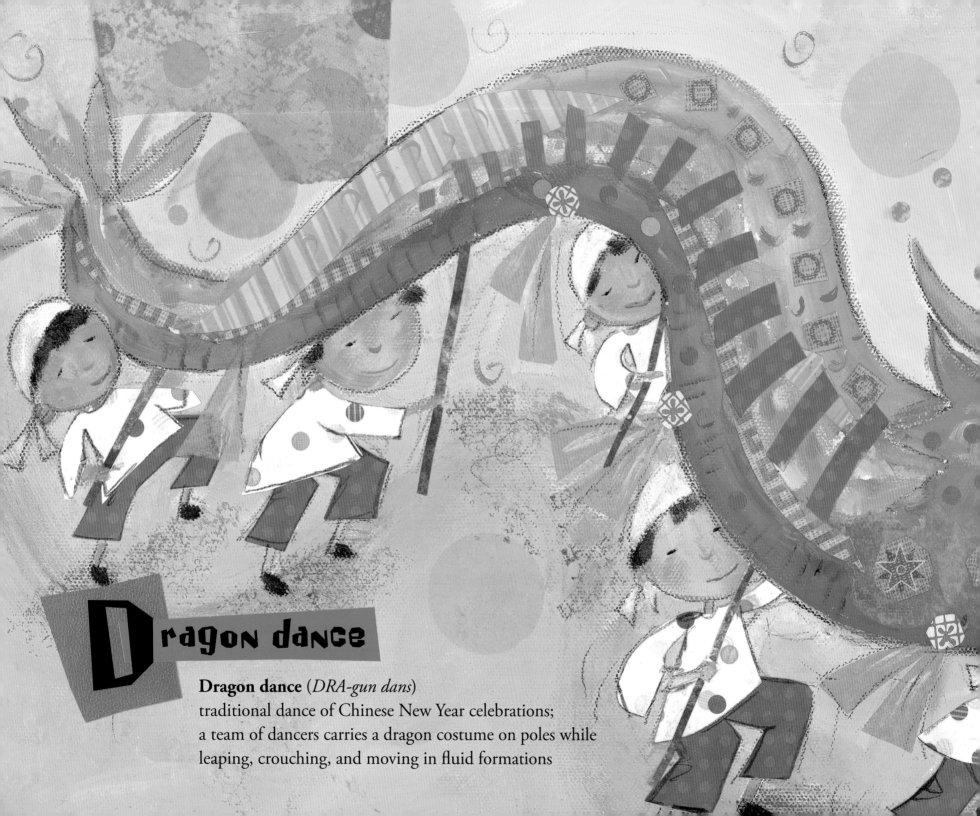

Dragon dance

Dragon dance (*DRA-gun dans*)
traditional dance of Chinese New Year celebrations;
a team of dancers carries a dragon costume on poles while
leaping, crouching, and moving in fluid formations

Energetic (*en-ur-JE-tik*)
full of lots of activity,
as in break dancing
or tap dancing

Energetic

Folk dance

Folk dance (*foke dans*) informal, traditional dance, such as the polka or the hora or the jig, performed at social gatherings

Gallop (*GAL-up*) a lively folk dance involving short, hopping steps

Gallop

Hula (*HOO-lah*)
a traditional Hawaiian dance;
dancers make graceful hand
motions while swaying
their hips

Hula

JUMP

Jump (*juhmp*)
a leap in the air,
which usually
changes the
position of the
feet upon landing

Improvisation

Improvisation
(*im-pro-vi-ZAY-shuhn*)
making up the steps as
one dances

Kick (*kik*)
a rhythmic and
powerful motion
of the legs

Kick

Leotard

Leotard
(*LEE-o-tahrd*)
a one-piece garment
covering the entire
torso

Music (*MYU-zik*)
sounds organized to form a rhythm,
melody, and harmony

Notation (*no-TAY-shuhn*)
in music or dance, a way of writing down
the sounds or steps so they can be read

Ouvert (*oo-VAIR*)
a French word that refers to an
open position of the feet in ballet

Position
(*poh-ZI-shuhn*)
placement of the feet
for performing a
ballet step; there are
five basic placements,
with corresponding
arrangements of
the arms

Position

Quickstep (*KWIK-step*)
fast ballroom dance that includes
hops, runs, quick steps, and turns

Quickstep

Recital (*ree-SY-tull*)
a performance given by
dancers or musicians

Stage

Stage (*stayj*)
the part of a theater on which
a performance takes place;
parts of the stage include the
wings (the sides of the stage
not visible to the audience),
the set (painted backgrounds,
rooms, furniture), the curtain,
and the lights (spotlights,
footlights)

Tap Dance

Tap Dance (*tap dans*)
lively, rhythmic dancing performed with small metal plates attached to the heels and toes of a pair of shoes to make a tapping sound

Upbeat/Downbeat
(*UP-beet/DOWN-beet*)
the upbeat is the last beat in a measure of music, the downbeat is the first and strongest beat

Upbeat/Downbeat

Variation (*vayr-ee-AY-shuhn*)
a solo dance in classical ballet

Variation

Warm-up (*WARM-up*)
series of stretches
and exercises to get the
muscles ready before
dancing

Warm-up

eXtension (*ik-STEN-shuhn*)
raising and holding the leg
high in the air

e**X**tension

Yearn (*yurn*)
to wish for something,
such as *yearning* to wear toe shoes
or be a ballet dancer

Zones

Zones (*zohns*)

different sections of the body

Shoulder Zone goes from the shoulders down to the bottom of the ribs.

Center Zone ties everything together by overlapping the lower edge of the rib cage and the upper tip of the hips.

Hip Zone covers the top of the hipbone down to where the hip socket connects to the leg.

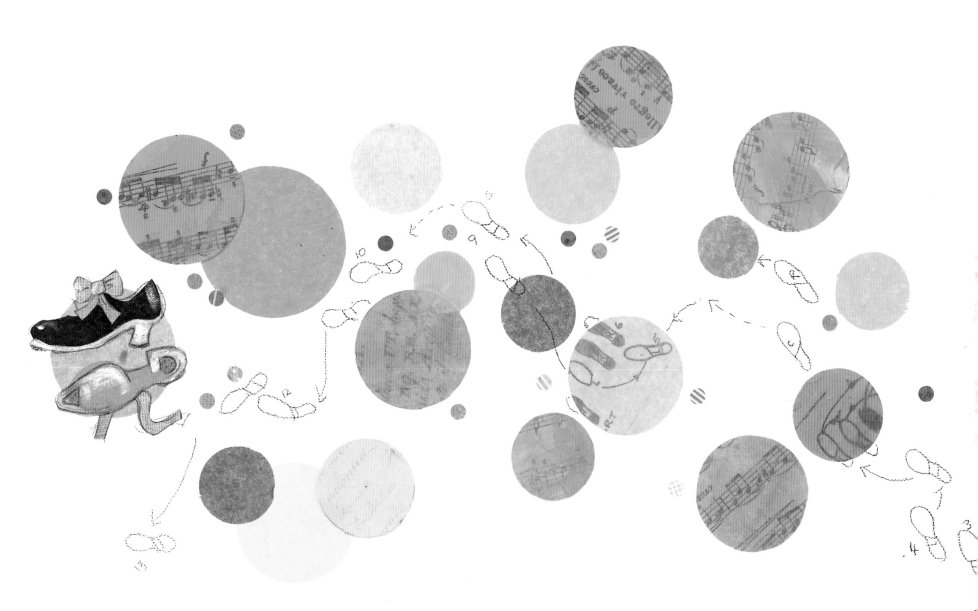

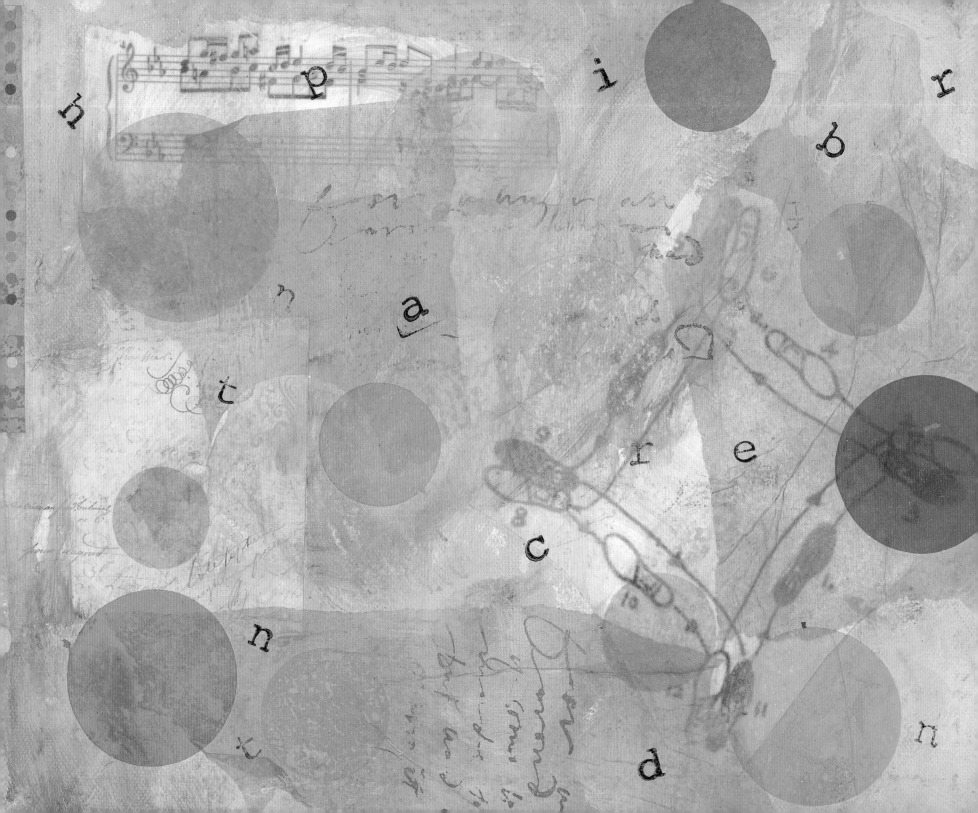